SILAGE MASTERY

Reduce Waste, Maximise Milk Production, and Boost Dairy Efficiency

—— First Ever Book on Baled Silage ——

SILAGE MASTERY

Reduce Waste, Maximise Milk Production, and Boost Dairy Efficiency

Garvit Garg

Worldwide Published by
Pendown Press

PENDOWN PRESS LLP

An ISO 9001 & ISO 14001 Certified Co.,

Regd. Office: 3767A, Kanhaiya Nagar,

Tri Nagar, Delhi-110035

Ph.: 8130886000, 9650072927

E-mail: info@pendownpress.com

Branch Office: 1A/2A, 20, Hari Sadan, Ansari Road,

Daryaganj, New Delhi-110002

Ph.: 011-45794768

Website: PendownPress.com

Edition: 2025

Price: ₹ 299

ISBN: 978-93-6338-421-7

Layout and Cover Designed by Pendown Graphics Team
Printed and Bound in India by Thomson Press India Ltd.

To all the hardworking dairy farmers and industry professionals of India. Your dedication and effort are what keep our country strong. I hope this book helps you grow and succeed, bringing better opportunities to you, your families, and our nation. Here's to a bright future for all the farmers of India.

Table of Contents

Acknowledgements

I am thrilled to present **"SILAGE MASTERY: REDUCE WASTE, MAXIMISE MILK PRODUCTION, AND BOOST DAIRY EFFICIENCY."** This book is a culmination of my expertise and experience in the field of silage film manufacturing, and it is with immense gratitude that I share it with you. I would like to extend my heartfelt appreciation to the individuals who have played a pivotal role in shaping my journey.

First and foremost, I would like to express my deepest gratitude to my father, **Mr. Adv. Gian Parkash Garg**, whose unwavering support and guidance have been instrumental in my professional growth. His wisdom and entrepreneurial spirit have inspired me to push boundaries and pursue excellence in the field of Silage film.

I would also like to thank my mother, **Mrs. Urmil Garg**, whose love and encouragement have been a constant source of motivation. Her unwavering belief in my abilities has given me the confidence to pursue my passion and make a difference in the dairy industry.

To my loving wife **Nitisha**, I am indebted for her patience, understanding, and unwavering support throughout the writing process. Her belief in my vision and tireless encouragement have fueled my determination to create a valuable resource for dairy farmers and industry professionals.

I would be remiss not to acknowledge my son, **Arkin**, whose infectious curiosity and boundless energy remind me of the importance of pushing the boundaries of knowledge and innovation. His presence in my life has been a constant reminder of the impact our work can have on future generations.

Furthermore, I owe a debt of gratitude to my esteemed Guru, **Mr. Akshar Yadav**. His profound wisdom, guidance, and mentorship have been instrumental in shaping my expertise and inspiring me to undertake the endeavor of writing this book. I am deeply grateful for his unwavering support and for instilling in me a passion for continuous learning and growth.

To my friend, **Mr. Dinesh Verma**, CEO of Pendown Press, and his team, who supported us throughout this creative process and provided great suggestions.

I extend my appreciation to all the dairy farmers, industry professionals, and experts who have shared their insights and experiences, contributing to the knowledge and wisdom presented within these pages. Your expertise and dedication to the dairy industry have been invaluable in shaping the content of this book.

Lastly, I want to express my sincere gratitude to the readers. It is your unwavering enthusiasm for learning and your commitment to driving progress in the dairy industry that has motivated me to put my thoughts and experiences into words. It is my fervent hope that **"Silage Mastery"** will serve as a source of inspiration and practical guidance as you seek to optimise your dairy productivity and achieve greater success.

With gratitude and humility, I present **"SILAGE MASTERY: REDUCE WASTE, MAXIMISE MILK PRODUCTION, AND BOOST DAIRY EFFICIENCY."** May it serve as a catalyst for positive change, leading to higher milk output, improved animal nutrition, and increased profitability in your dairy business.

Garvit Garg

Expert in Silage Film Manufacturing

About the Author - Garvit Garg

Garvit Garg, born into a farming family, has always felt a strong connection to the land and the farming community. Growing up surrounded by Mehandi and Wheat farms, he witnessed firsthand the challenges faced by farmers. This early exposure ignited a deep passion within him to make a positive difference in the lives of his fellow farmers.

After completing his studies, Garvit set out on a mission to learn more about the problems faced by farmers across India. He wanted to find practical solutions that could improve their lives. During his journey, he discovered the immense potential of silage as a way to enhance feed quality and reduce agricultural waste. This realization led him to focus on producing silage films, a key component in preserving silage.

In 2016, Garvit took a brave step and started his own silage film production unit. However, his first attempt didn't go as planned, and the product didn't meet expectations. It was disheartening, and Garvit contemplated giving up on his dream. But a conversation with a close friend reminded him of his greater purpose – to serve the country and its farmers.

Determined to succeed, Garvit dedicated himself to research and development, spending countless hours improving his silage film. His hard work paid off in 2017 when a European client approved his product, impressed by his commitment to quality.

However, Garvit's goal extended beyond just providing a product. He wanted to offer farmers valuable insights and support to help them increase their profits. By listening to farmers and understanding their needs, Garvit became a trusted advisor, earning the affectionate title of "Garvit Bhai" among the farming community.

Realizing the power of sharing his knowledge, Garvit decided to write a book on silage. This book aims to empower farmers, clients, and researchers with a practical guide to mastering silage, offering a wealth of information in a simple and accessible language. Through this book, Garvit wants to support sustainable and profitable farming practices while showing his genuine care for the welfare of Indian farmers.

In addition to his work in the silage industry, Garvit is the creator of the popular YouTube channel, "Agro Mastery with Garvit". Through his channel, he shares valuable insights, tips, and in-depth knowledge on agricultural practices, silage management, and dairy business challenges, making him a trusted voice in the agricultural community.

Garvit Garg's journey from facing initial setbacks to achieving remarkable success is a powerful testament to his resilience and deep commitment to serving farmers. In this book, he shares not only his technical expertise but also the compassion and genuine concern that drives his dedication to the farming community. Garvit's unwavering spirit and his heartfelt desire to help farmers shine through these pages, establishing him as both a trusted authority and a true friend to the farming community.

Introduction

"Silage Mastery" is a comprehensive guide that explores the critical role of silage film in the dairy industry and its impact on optimising productivity and profitability. Authored by Garvit Garg, a leading expert in silage film manufacturing, this book delves into the various aspects of silage production, preservation, and utilisation.

The book begins by providing a detailed overview of silage and its significance as a vital feed source for dairy farms. It highlights the importance of high-quality silage in maximising milk production and ensuring optimal nutrition for livestock. The chapters outline the benefits of using silage film to preserve forage and maintain its nutrient value, leading to higher productivity of milk from cows.

The book further explores the different types of silage film available in the market and the key factors to consider when selecting the appropriate film for specific farm requirements. It also uncovers the science behind silage film production, shedding light on the raw materials and manufacturing processes that define quality. Readers will gain valuable knowledge about the various types of UV stabilisers and additives used in silage film production and their impact on UV protection, film durability, and longevity.

As you progress through the chapters, Garvit Garg emphasises the many advantages of using advanced film techniques, such as reduced film usage and improved wrapping methods, to minimise packing costs and maximise the number of bales per roll. The chapters provide practical tips and techniques for achieving optimal silage compaction, reducing spoilage, and ensuring consistent feed availability throughout the year.

The book also delves into the innovative technology of Printed Silage Film, which enables branding and marketing opportunities for farmers. It explores the advantages of printed film in creating brand visibility and enhancing customer engagement.

To illustrate the real-world applications of silage film, the author presents a series of engaging case studies. These success stories feature dairy farmers and livestock producers who faced specific challenges and successfully overcame them through the effective use of silage film. Each case study demonstrates the positive outcomes achieved, such as improved forage preservation, enhanced animal health, and increased farm profitability.

By the end of the book, readers will have gained a comprehensive understanding of silage film and its crucial role in optimising dairy productivity. Armed with valuable knowledge and practical insights, dairy business owners and industry professionals can make informed decisions about selecting, using, and leveraging silage film to strengthen their operations and boost profitability.

"Silage Mastery" is a must-read for anyone involved in the dairy industry. Whether you are a farmer, consultant, or industry professional, this book offers a wealth of information and actionable insights that will help you increase milk output, improve animal nutrition, and drive success in your business.

CHAPTER 1

Introduction to Silage:
The Foundation of Dairy Productivity

1.1 The Significance of Silage in Dairy Farming

Silage plays a vital role in the dairy industry as a key component of a cow's diet. It serves as a nutrient-rich feed source that provides essential energy, proteins, vitamins, and minerals necessary for maintaining optimal cow health and maximising milk production. Unlike fresh forage, silage offers year-round availability, making it a reliable and cost-effective choice for dairy farmers.

The ability to preserve forage as silage revolutionized the way farmers manage feed resources. Silage ensures that an abundant supply of high-quality feed is accessible even during times of limited grazing or unfavorable weather conditions. By providing a consistent and nutritious diet, silage contributes to the overall productivity and well-being of dairy cows.

1.2 Historical Background and Evolution of Silage Preservation

The practice of silage preservation dates back centuries, with early methods involving the use of pits or trenches covered with straw, leaves, or soil to exclude oxygen and facilitate fermentation. These rudimentary techniques, while somewhat effective, had limitations in terms of quality control and consistency, often resulting in variable feed quality.

The 19th century marked the beginning of significant advancements in silage preservation. Pioneers in the field introduced innovations such as silos, airtight storage structures that allowed better control over the fermentation process. As scientific understanding grew, the role of lactic acid bacteria in silage fermentation was discovered, leading to more controlled and efficient preservation techniques. These innovations laid the foundation for the modern silage production practices that are essential to today's dairy farming success.

1.3 The Science Behind Silage Fermentation

Silage fermentation is a natural biological process that transforms fresh forage, such as grass, legumes, or corn—into a preserved, nutrient-rich feed under anaerobic conditions. The process begins when plant sugars are broken down by lactic acid bacteria, which convert these sugars into lactic acid through a series of intricate biochemical reactions. The lactic acid acts as a natural preservative, lowering the pH of the silage and creating an environment that inhibits the growth of harmful microorganisms, ensuring the long-term preservation of forage quality.

The success of silage fermentation depends on several key factors:

➤ **Moisture Content:** Optimal levels support bacterial activity while preventing undesirable spoilage.

➤ **Sugar Availability:** Adequate sugars are essential to fuel the fermentation process.

➤ **Plant Maturity:** Harvesting forage at the right stage ensures maximum nutrient density and enhances fermentation efficiency.

➤ **Compaction:** Proper compaction eliminates air pockets, creating the anaerobic conditions required for lactic acid bacteria to thrive.

Mastering these factors is crucial to achieving well-fermented silage that retains its nutritional value and provides consistent benefits to dairy operations.

1.4 Nutritional Value of Well-Preserved Silage

Well-preserved silage offers numerous nutritional benefits for dairy cows. Fermentation enhances the digestibility of fibrous materials, breaking down complex carbohydrates into simpler forms that can be more readily absorbed by the cow's digestive system. This increased digestibility translates into improved feed efficiency and nutrient utilization, supporting optimal milk production.

Nutritional Values	
Dry Matter	32% (±3%)
Crude Protein	7 - 9%
ADF	25 - 35%
NDF	35 - 50%
Energy	20 - 25%
pH	3.7 - 4.2

Silage also retains a significant portion of the forage's original nutritional composition. It provides essential energy sources, including carbohydrates and fats, along with proteins, vitamins, and minerals. This comprehensive nutrient profile ensures a well-balanced diet for dairy cows, contributing to their overall health, milk quality, and productivity.

1.5 Challenges and Considerations in Silage Production

While silage offers many benefits, its production comes with some challenges that need careful management to get the best results.

> **Managing Moisture:** Getting the right moisture content at harvest is very important. Forage that's too wet can lead to over-fermentation, causing nutrient loss, reduced taste, and spoilage due to harmful bacteria. If the forage is too dry,

fermentation may not happen properly, which can lower the nutritional value.

➢ **Harvest Timing:** Forage must be harvested at the right stage to lock in its nutrients. Younger forage usually has more protein and energy, so timing is key to capturing its peak quality. Delaying the harvest can reduce its digestibility and overall feed value.

➢ **Proper Storage and Packing:** Good storage practices, like tightly packing silage to remove air, are necessary to create the oxygen-free conditions needed for fermentation. Poor storage can lead to mold, spoilage, and financial loss.

With the right knowledge, planning, and attention to detail, farmers can handle these challenges and make the most of their silage. This ensures high-quality feed for their cows, leading to better productivity and farm profitability.

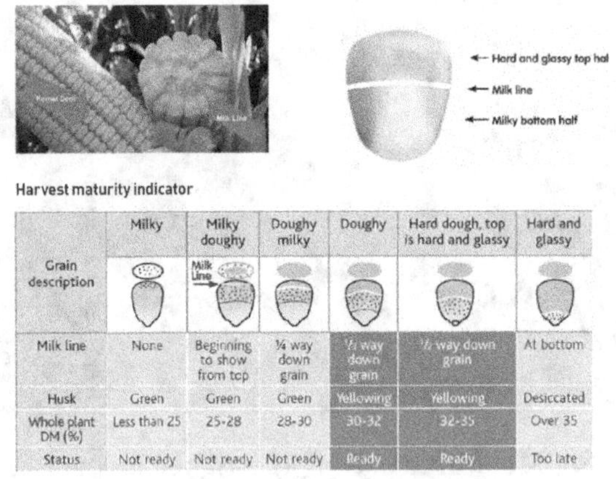

	Milky	Milky doughy	Doughy milky	Doughy	Hard dough, top is hard and glassy	Hard and glassy
Grain description						
Milk line	None	Beginning to show from top	¼ way down grain	½ way down grain	¾ way down grain	At bottom
Husk	Green	Green	Green	Yellowing	Yellowing	Desiccated
Whole plant DM (%)	Less than 25	25-28	28-30	30-32	32-35	Over 35
Status	Not ready	Not ready	Not ready	Ready	Ready	Too late

Harvest Maturity Indicator

CHAPTER 2

The Science Behind Silage: Fermentation and Nutritional Value

2.1 Understanding the Fermentation Process in Silage

Silage fermentation is a complex biological process driven by lactic acid bacteria. Understanding the key steps of this process is crucial for producing high-quality silage. The fermentation process begins as soon as fresh forage is ensiled and oxygen is removed. Lactic acid bacteria, either naturally present on the plant material or added as inoculants, start to consume sugars and produce lactic acid through anaerobic respiration.

Figure 1 Six phases of silage fermentation and storage

Phase I	Phase II	Phase III	Phase IV	Phase V	Phase VI
Cell respiration production of CO_2 heat and water	Production of acetic acid and lactic acid ethanol	Lactic acid formation	Lactic acid formation	Material storage	Aerobic decomposition on re-exposure to oxygen
69° F	90° F		84° F		84° F
Temp change					
6.0 - 6.5	5.0		4.0		7.0
pH change					
	Acetic acid and lactic acid bacteria	Lactic acid bacteria	Lactic acid bacteria		Mold and yeast activity

2   3   4   21

Age of silage (days)

As the lactic acid builds up, the pH of the silage decreases, creating an acidic environment. This acidity inhibits the growth of spoilage-causing bacteria and molds, preserving the forage and maintaining its nutritional value. Proper fermentation relies on factors such as temperature, moisture content, compaction, and exclusion of oxygen, which collectively support the growth and activity of lactic acid bacteria.

2.2 The Role of Lactic Acid Bacteria in Silage Fermentation

Lactic acid bacteria (LAB) are the primary microorganisms responsible for silage fermentation. They convert the sugars present in the forage into lactic acid, creating a favorable acidic environment that preserves the silage. Different species of LAB, such as Lactobacillus and Pediococcus, contribute to the fermentation process and play a role in determining the quality and characteristics of the silage.

LAB thrive under anaerobic conditions, where oxygen is limited, making proper sealing and compaction crucial for their growth. These bacteria utilize the sugars in the forage, including glucose and fructose, as their energy source. Through their metabolic activity, LAB not only produces lactic acid but also generates other organic acids, such as acetic acid and propionic acid, which further contribute to silage preservation.

2.3 Factors Influencing Silage Quality and Fermentation

The success of silage fermentation depends on several critical factors:

> **Moisture Content:** Forage moisture must be within an optimal range. Too much moisture can lead to nutrient loss from seepage and undesirable byproducts, while too little moisture hinders bacterial growth and fermentation.

> **Sugar Availability:** Sugars fuel LAB, and higher sugar content in forage ensures efficient fermentation. Forages harvested at earlier maturity stages typically contain more sugars, leading to faster and better fermentation.

> **Compaction:** Properly compacted forage removes oxygen, creating the ideal anaerobic environment for LAB to thrive. Poor compaction can leave air pockets that encourage spoilage and lower silage quality.

Farmers must carefully balance these factors to produce high-quality silage that supports livestock health and productivity.

2.4 Optimizing Silage Fermentation for Nutritional Value

Optimizing silage fermentation is essential to preserving the forage's nutritional value and ensuring its effectiveness as livestock feed. Proper fermentation enhances the digestibility of fibrous components, making nutrients more accessible to the cow's digestive system. This improved nutrient availability increases feed efficiency, directly contributing to higher milk production and better overall animal health.

To achieve optimal fermentation:

➤ **Seal Storage Structures Airtight:** Proper sealing of silos or bunkers is vital to exclude oxygen, which can cause undesirable aerobic fermentation and nutrient loss.

➤ **Compact Forage Adequately:** Effective compaction eliminates air pockets, creating the anaerobic conditions necessary for lactic acid bacteria (LAB) to thrive and work efficiently.

➤ **Use Microbial Inoculants:** Adding inoculants with carefully selected strains of LAB can significantly boost fermentation quality. These beneficial bacteria outcompete spoilage organisms, ensuring consistent results and superior silage preservation.

By understanding the science behind silage fermentation, dairy farmers can make strategic choices to refine their silage production practices. Techniques like proper sealing, compaction, and inoculant use help maximize the silage's nutritional potential.

Ultimately, high-quality silage serves as the foundation for healthier livestock, greater milk yields, and improved profitability in dairy operations. With attention to these key steps, farmers can harness the full benefits of well-preserved forage.

CHAPTER 3

Silage Film: Preserving Quality for Maximum Nutritional Benefit

3.1 The Role of Silage Film in Silage Preservation

Silage film is a crucial component in the preservation of high-quality silage. Its primary purpose is to create an airtight seal around the silage, preventing the entry of oxygen and moisture, which can compromise fermentation and lead to spoilage. Silage film acts as a protective barrier, shielding the ensiled forage from external factors that can degrade its nutritional value.

By tightly wrapping the silage bales or covering the silo surface, silage film plays a vital role in maintaining anaerobic conditions. It provides a physical barrier that keeps oxygen out and allows the fermentation process to occur efficiently. This helps to preserve the essential nutrients and promote the production of lactic acid, contributing to the overall quality of the silage.

3.2 Characteristics of High-Quality Silage Film

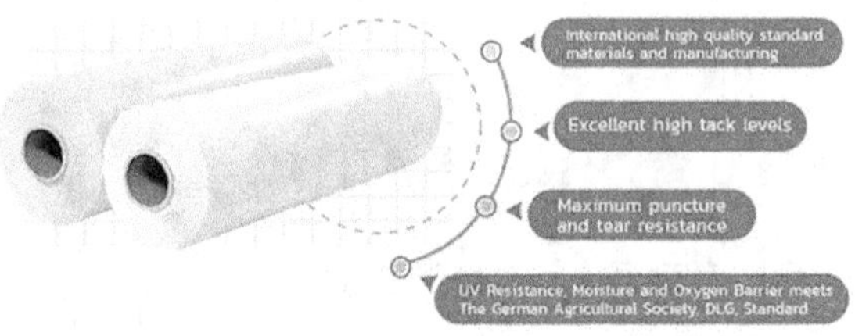

To ensure effective silage preservation, it is essential to select a high-quality silage film that meets specific criteria. Some key characteristics of a reliable silage film include:

Thickness and Strength: A durable and tear-resistant silage film is essential to withstand the rigors of storage and handling. The film should have sufficient thickness to protect against punctures or tears during wrapping, unwrapping, or transportation, ensuring long-lasting performance.

Oxygen and Moisture Barrier: An effective silage film should have excellent barrier properties, preventing the entry of oxygen and moisture into the silage. This ensures that the anaerobic conditions required for proper fermentation are maintained, reducing the risk of spoilage and nutrient degradation.

UV Protection: UV radiation from sunlight can degrade the quality of silage by breaking down essential nutrients and reducing palatability. A high-quality silage film should have UV stabilizers incorporated into its composition, providing protection against UV radiation and extending the shelf life of the silage.

Stretchability: The ability of the silage film to stretch and conform tightly to the bales or silo surface is crucial for achieving proper compaction and sealing. Stretchability helps to eliminate air pockets and ensure a secure and uniform coverage, optimizing the preservation process.

Easy Application and Removal: User-friendly features such as ease of handling, cutting, and wrapping make the application and removal of the silage film more efficient. This saves time and labor during the silage-making process.

3.3 Advances in Silage Film Technology

Over the years, significant advancements have been made in silage film technology to enhance its performance and effectiveness in silage preservation. These innovations focus on improving key attributes such as strength, oxygen barrier properties, UV resistance, and stretchability, addressing challenges faced by modern dairy operations.

High Quality Silage Film Making Technology

Manufacturers have developed **multi-layered silage** films that combine different materials to optimize the film's strength, tear resistance, and barrier properties. These multilayer films provide enhanced protection against oxygen and moisture ingress, ensuring better preservation of the silage's nutritional value.

The incorporation of advanced UV stabilizers into silage films ensures exceptional resistance to sunlight-induced degradation. This innovation not only prevents the breakdown of essential nutrients but also extends the silage's shelf life, even in regions with high UV radiation levels. As a result, farmers can confidently store silage for longer durations without compromising quality, improving the reliability of their feed supply.

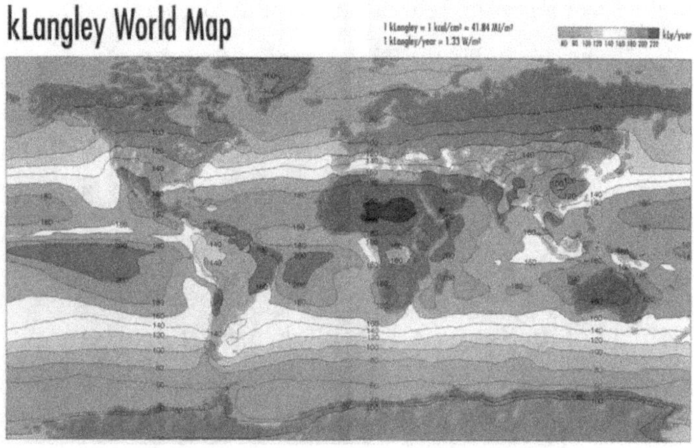

UV Radiation Level around the world

Furthermore, advancements in film extrusion technology have enabled the production of thinner yet highly durable films. These thinner films offer improved stretchability, allowing for tighter and more secure wrapping, which enhances compaction and preservation.

3.4 Best Practices in Silage Film Application

To maximize the benefits of silage film, proper application techniques should be followed. Some best practices include:

Ensuring Proper Film Coverage: The silage film should be applied in a manner that provides complete coverage of the bales or silo surface, leaving no gaps or exposed areas. This ensures effective sealing and prevents oxygen ingress.

Applying Sufficient Layers: Applying multiple layers of silage film can provide added protection and strengthen the overall barrier against oxygen and moisture. Following the manufacturer's recommendations for the number of film layers is important to achieve optimal preservation.

Securing Film Edges: Properly securing the edges of the silage film helps to prevent wind damage or loosening of the film during storage. This can be done using specialized edge sealing or weighting systems, ensuring the film remains intact and airtight.

Monitoring Film Integrity: Regularly inspecting the silage film for any signs of damage, such as punctures or tears, is essential. Damaged areas should be repaired or replaced promptly to maintain effective preservation.

By following these best practices and utilizing the advancements in silage film technology, dairy farmers can confidently preserve their silage's quality and maximize the nutritional benefits for their livestock.

Looking Ahead

As the dairy industry continues to evolve and strive for higher productivity, understanding the importance of silage film and implementing proper preservation techniques is crucial. The next chapter will explore the impact of high-quality silage and film preservation on milk production and the overall success of dairy businesses.

CHAPTER 4

Maximizing Milk Production through High
Quality Silage and Film Preservation

4.1 The Link Between Silage Quality and Milk Production

The quality of silage plays a significant role in the overall productivity and performance of dairy cows. Silage serves as a crucial component of their diet, providing essential nutrients and energy for milk production. When cows consume high-quality silage, they receive a balanced and nutritious feed that directly impacts their milk production.

Proper fermentation and preservation of silage ensure the retention of essential nutrients such as proteins, carbohydrates, and vitamins. These nutrients contribute to the overall health and well being of dairy cows, supporting optimal milk production. In contrast, silage that undergoes inefficient fermentation or is exposed to spoilage can result in reduced nutrient availability and suboptimal milk production.

4.2 The Role of Silage Film in Preserving Nutritional Value

Silage film plays a critical role in preserving the nutritional value of silage. By creating an airtight seal around the ensiled forage, it prevents the entry of oxygen, which can lead to spoilage and nutrient degradation. The use of high-quality silage film ensures that the fermentation process occurs under anaerobic conditions, preserving the essential nutrients and maximizing their availability for the cows.

UV protection provided by the silage film is equally important. Ultraviolet radiation from sunlight can break down essential nutrients in silage, ultimately reducing its nutritional value. Silage films with UV stabilizers effectively block harmful UV rays, extending the shelf life of the silage while maintaining its nutritional integrity and ensuring that it remains a valuable resource for dairy cows.

4.3 Improved Silage Quality and Milk Production

When dairy farmers implement proper silage preservation techniques using high-quality silage film, the impact on milk production can be significant. Here are some key benefits:

Enhanced Nutrient Availability: High-quality silage with its preserved nutrients translates into a more balanced and nutrient-rich diet for dairy cows. This promotes their overall health and well-being, leading to improved milk production.

Consistent Feed Quality: Silage that is well-preserved and protected by the silage film maintains consistent feed quality throughout the year. This ensures that cows receive a consistent diet, minimizing fluctuations in milk production and ensuring steady output.

Increased Dry Matter Intake: Good silage quality and preservation contribute to increased dry matter intake by dairy cows. Higher dry matter intake allows cows to consume more nutrients, which positively impacts milk production.

Improved Digestibility: Properly preserved silage is more digestible for cows, resulting in better utilization of the nutrients it contains. Improved digestibility promotes efficient feed conversion, optimizing milk production.

Stable Rumen Environment: High-quality silage helps maintain a stable rumen environment, promoting healthy rumen function. A healthy rumen supports optimal digestion and nutrient absorption, which directly impacts milk production.

4.4 Success Stories: Dairy Farms and Increased Milk Production

Numerous dairy farms have witnessed significant improvements in milk production by focusing on high-quality silage and film preservation. Here are a few success stories:

Green Acres Dairy: By implementing stringent silage preservation practices, including the use of top-quality silage film, Green Acres Dairy achieved a 10% increase in milk production within just six months. The improved nutritional value of the silage resulted in healthier cows and higher milk yields.

Sunnydale Farm: After switching to a superior silage film with advanced oxygen barrier properties, Sunnydale Farm experienced reduced spoilage and improved silage quality. This led to a 15% increase in milk production and improved overall farm profitability.

Meadowview Dairy: Meadowview Dairy focused on optimizing their silage-making process, including proper compaction and precise application of silage film. These efforts resulted in more consistent silage quality, leading to a 12% increase in milk production and improved milk components.

These success stories demonstrate the direct correlation between high-quality silage, effective film preservation, and increased milk production. By implementing similar techniques and utilizing advanced silage film, dairy farmers can unlock the full potential of their operations.

In the next chapter, we will explore the economic benefits of investing in high-quality silage and film preservation, highlighting the positive impact on dairy farm profitability.

CHAPTER 5

The Economic Benefits of High-Quality Silage and Film Preservation

5.1 Understanding the Economic Impact

In the dairy industry, profitability is a key consideration for dairy farmers. Maximizing milk production while minimizing costs is essential for a sustainable and thriving business. This chapter explores the significant economic benefits that stem from utilizing high-quality silage and effective film preservation techniques.

5.2 Improved Feed Efficiency

One of the primary economic benefits of high-quality silage and film preservation is improved feed efficiency. When cows consume nutrient-dense and well-preserved silage, their digestion and nutrient utilization are optimized. This leads to increased milk production per unit of feed consumed, resulting in improved feed efficiency. By maximizing the nutritional value of each pound of silage, dairy farmers can reduce their overall feed costs and achieve higher milk production without compromising the cow's health.

5.3 Reduced Feed Costs

High-quality silage, preserved effectively with the right film, helps minimize feed losses and wastage. When silage is properly preserved using the right film, spoilage and degradation are minimized, ensuring that more of the harvested forage is available for feed. This reduces the need to purchase additional feed and lowers overall feed costs for the dairy farm. By minimizing feed losses and optimizing feed utilization, dairy farmers can achieve significant cost savings over time while maintaining a consistent level of high-quality feed for their herd.

5.4 Enhanced Animal Health and Reduced Veterinary Expenses

Properly preserved silage, rich in essential nutrients, promotes the health and well-being of dairy cows. When cows receive a balanced and high-quality diet, their immune systems become stronger, reducing the risk of diseases and health issues. This, in turn, leads to reduced veterinary expenses, including costs associated with treatments and medications. By investing in high-quality silage and film preservation, dairy farmers can proactively manage the health of their herd and save on veterinary expenses, contributing to long-term savings.

5.5 Increased Milk Production and Revenue

The ultimate goal of any dairy farmer is to achieve higher milk production and, consequently, increased revenue. High-quality silage and effective film preservation directly contribute to enhanced milk production. Improved feed efficiency, optimal nutrient utilization, and consistent feed quality result in higher milk yields from each cow. This increased milk production translates into higher revenue for the dairy farm, improving its overall profitability and sustainability.

5.6 Case Studies: Financial Success through Silage and Film Preservation

Several case studies showcase the financial success achieved by dairy farms that prioritize high-quality silage and film preservation:

Maple Grove Dairy: By implementing a comprehensive silage management program and utilizing superior silage film, Maple Grove Dairy achieved a 20% increase in milk production. The revenue boost from this improvement significantly enhanced their financial performance, enabling further investments in farm operations.

Meadowland Farms: Meadowland Farms made strategic investments in advanced film preservation technology, resulting in reduced spoilage and improved silage quality. As a result, they saw a 15% increase in milk production and a corresponding increase in revenue, strengthening the farm's financial position.

Sunnybrook Dairy: Through careful attention to silage quality and effective film preservation, Sunnybrook Dairy achieved a 10% reduction in feed costs while simultaneously increasing milk production by 12%. This led to substantial financial savings and improved profitability.

These case studies illustrate the tangible economic benefits that dairy farms can experience by prioritizing high-quality silage and effective film preservation techniques.

In the next chapter, we will delve into the environmental advantages of silage and film preservation, highlighting the sustainability and resource efficiency aspects that contribute to a greener dairy industry.

○ ○ ○ ○

CHAPTER 6

Innovations in Silage Film Technology:
Introducing Printed Silage Film

6.1 Introduction to Printed Silage Film

In recent years, the silage film industry has witnessed remarkable advancements driven by cutting-edge technology and a focus on improving preservation techniques. These innovations have led to the introduction of new products that not only enhance the functionality of silage wrapping but also open up exciting opportunities for branding and marketing. One such breakthrough is Printed Silage Film, which offers a combination of functionality and branding opportunities. In this chapter, we explore the features and benefits of this revolutionary product and its impact on the industry.

6.2 The Advantages of Printed Silage Film

Printed Silage Film retains all the essential properties of traditional silage film, providing superior UV protection and preservation capabilities. What sets it apart is the additional feature of customization, allowing for the inclusion of logos, designs, or messages directly printed on the film. This offers unique branding and marketing opportunities for farmers and agricultural businesses, making their silage bales visually appealing and impactful.

6.3 Branding and Marketing Possibilities

The introduction of Printed Silage Film opens up new avenues for branding and marketing within the agricultural sector. By incorporating their logos, product names, or promotional messages on the film, businesses can enhance their brand visibility and create a distinct identity in the market. Each wrapped bale becomes a powerful marketing asset, effectively promoting the brand and capturing attention within the agricultural landscape.

6.4 Product Differentiation and Customer Engagement

Customized Printed Silage Film enables businesses to differentiate their products and stand out from competitors. By utilizing unique designs, colors, or messages on the film, companies can create a lasting impression among customers and enhance customer engagement. This differentiation not only attracts attention but also fosters brand loyalty and drives business growth.

6.5 Practical Applications and Success Stories

Numerous farmers and agricultural businesses have successfully leveraged Printed Silage Film to elevate their marketing efforts.

Whether displaying logos, taglines, or important farm-related information, these customized films have proven to be effective tools in increasing brand recognition, attracting customer inquiries, and driving sales. As a result, businesses have witnessed improved market presence and growth, highlighting the tangible benefits of incorporating this innovative technology into their operations.

6.6 Environmental Considerations

Despite the additional printing process, Printed Silage Film remains environmentally conscious. Manufacturers employ eco-friendly printing technologies and utilize inks that are safe for the environment and do not compromise the quality of the ensiled forage. Additionally, the film is fully recyclable, aligning with sustainable practices and promoting environmental responsibility within the agricultural industry. This balance between innovation and sustainability underscores the broader commitment to responsible agricultural practices.

In the next chapter, we will explore the future possibilities of silage film technology and discuss ongoing advancements and research that will continue to shape the industry.

○　○　○　○

CHAPTER 7

The Future of Silage Film Technology

7.1 Advancements in Film Composition

As the demand for high-quality silage continues to grow, the need for advanced film compositions has become paramount. This chapter explores the latest advancements in film composition, focusing on materials that offer improved strength, flexibility, and barrier properties. Researchers and manufacturers are continuously working on new polymers, additives, and blending techniques to develop films that provide enhanced performance and longevity ensuring they meet the evolving needs of the agricultural industry.

7.2 Nano and Micro Technologies in Silage Films

Nano and micro technologies have gained significant attention in the field of silage film development. These technologies involve incorporating nanoparticles or microstructures into the film matrix to impart specific functionalities. In this chapter, we delve into the potential applications of these technologies, such as enhanced UV protection, oxygen barrier properties, and antimicrobial properties. The chapter discusses the ongoing research and potential benefits these technologies offer for the future of silage film.

7.3 Biodegradable and Eco-Friendly Film Solutions

Sustainability and environmental responsibility are increasingly important considerations in modern agriculture. This chapter explores the development of biodegradable and eco-friendly silage film solutions. These films are designed to break down naturally over time, reducing the environmental impact associated with traditional films. The chapter discusses the challenges and opportunities in developing biodegradable films and their potential for widespread adoption in the industry, as they align with global sustainability goals.

7.4 Smart Film Technologies for Enhanced Monitoring and Quality Control

The integration of smart technologies into silage films opens up new possibilities for monitoring and quality control. This chapter looks at advancements in smart film technologies, such as embedded sensors, RFID tags, and data collection systems. These technologies enable real-time monitoring of key parameters like temperature, humidity, and gas concentrations inside the silage bales. The chapter discusses the potential benefits of these technologies in ensuring optimal silage preservation and quality.

7.5 Predictive Modeling and Artificial Intelligence in Silage Preservation

Predictive modeling and artificial intelligence (AI) have the potential to revolutionize silage preservation. This chapter delves into how these technologies are being used to develop models that can predict silage quality and fermentation outcomes based on various factors such as crop type, moisture content, and environmental conditions. By combining these models with AI algorithms, farmers can gain valuable insights and recommendations to improve silage production and storage methods, ensuring higher-quality silage with less waste.

7.6 Innovations in Film Application and Wrapping Machinery

Film application and wrapping machinery play a crucial role in the efficient and effective use of silage film. In this chapter, we explore the latest innovations in film application and wrapping machinery, including advancements in automation, film stretching technologies, and wrapping speed control. These innovations aim to improve the ease of use, productivity, and consistency of film application, ensuring optimal coverage and minimizing film waste.

By exploring these advancements in silage film technology, Chapter 7 provides readers with insights into the future of the industry. The chapter highlights the ongoing research, emerging trends, and potential benefits these advancements offer in terms of silage preservation, environmental sustainability, and operational efficiency. Understanding these developments equips readers with the knowledge needed to stay ahead in an ever-evolving agricultural landscape.

Silage Film and Animal Nutrition

Chapter 8 explores the critical link between silage film and animal nutrition. It highlights how proper silage preservation using high-quality film directly impacts the nutritional value of ensiled forage and, consequently, the health and productivity of livestock. This chapter delves into various aspects related to silage film and animal nutrition, including:

8.1 Silage Fermentation and Nutrient Preservation

It begins by providing an in-depth understanding of the fermentation process that occurs during silage production. It explains how the use of high-quality silage film helps create anaerobic conditions necessary for efficient fermentation. The chapter explores the role of different microorganisms involved in the fermentation process and their impact on nutrient preservation. Readers will gain insights into how silage film contributes to maintaining the nutritional quality of ensiled forage by minimizing nutrient losses.

8.2 Ensiling Techniques for Optimal Nutrient Retention

This section focuses on the various ensiling techniques that ensure optimal nutrient retention. It discusses the importance of proper harvesting, chopping, and packing practices in maximizing nutrient preservation. The chapter highlights how the use of silage film acts as a barrier against air and moisture, preventing the growth of spoilage microorganisms and minimizing nutrient degradation. Readers will learn about the specific factors that influence nutrient retention during ensiling and how silage film plays a crucial role in preserving these valuable nutrients.

8.3 Effect of Silage Quality on Animal Health and Productivity

It explores the direct relationship between silage quality and animal health and productivity. It emphasizes how the nutritional content of silage affects the overall well-being and performance of livestock. The chapter discusses the impact of poor-quality silage, such as increased risk of metabolic disorders, reduced feed intake, and compromised production. On the other hand, it highlights the benefits of high-quality silage in terms of improved rumen function, enhanced nutrient utilization, and increased milk production. Readers will gain a deeper understanding of how silage film contributes to ensuring high-quality silage, ultimately benefiting animal health and productivity.

8.4 Evaluating Silage Quality for Nutritional Analysis

This section provides insights into evaluating silage quality for nutritional analysis. It discusses various methods and techniques used to assess the nutritional composition of silage, including laboratory analysis and near-infrared spectroscopy (NIRS). The chapter emphasizes the importance of accurate nutritional analysis in formulating balanced diets for livestock. Readers will gain knowledge on how silage film influences the consistency and reliability of nutritional analysis results by minimizing variability and preserving nutrient integrity.

8.5 Silage Film's Role in Ensuring High-Quality Animal Feed

The final section of this chapter highlights the pivotal role of silage film in providing high-quality animal feed. It discusses how the use of proper film ensures optimal silage preservation, resulting in a nutrient-rich and palatable feed source for livestock. The chapter emphasizes the importance of consistently delivering high-quality silage to meet the nutritional needs of animals throughout the year. Readers will understand how silage film contributes to ensuring a reliable and consistent supply of nutritious feed, thereby supporting optimal animal health, growth, and productivity.

By delving into the intricate connection between silage film and animal nutrition, Chapter 8 provides valuable insights for dairy business owners and livestock producers. The chapter underscores the significance of using high-quality silage film to preserve the nutritional integrity of ensiled forage, ultimately leading to improved animal health, productivity, and profitability.

○ ○ ○ ○

Silage Film and Operational Efficiency

Chapter 9 explores the crucial role of silage film in boosting operational efficiency within the dairy and livestock industry. It highlights how the right choice of silage film and its proper application can significantly streamline various aspects of silage production, storage, and feeding processes. This chapter delves into the following key areas:

9.1 Film Selection Criteria for Optimal Efficiency

Chapter 9 begins by discussing the essential criteria to consider when selecting silage film for optimal operational efficiency. It covers factors such as film thickness, width, and mechanical properties that impact film performance and application. The chapter provides guidelines for choosing the right film based on specific requirements, environmental conditions, and machinery capabilities. Readers will gain insights into how selecting the appropriate film contributes to efficient wrapping, reduced film waste, and improved overall operational efficiency.

9.2 Film Application Techniques and Equipment

This section focuses on film application techniques and equipment that enhance operational efficiency. It explores various methods such as individual bale wrapping, inline wrapping, and combination wrapping, highlighting their advantages and considerations. The chapter highlights cutting-edge advancements in wrapping machinery, such as automatic film dispensers, stretchers, and tension control systems, emphasizing their role in improving consistency and efficiency. Moreover, the chapter underscores the importance of regular equipment maintenance and calibration to ensure precise and optimal film application.

9.3 Minimizing Film Waste and Cost Optimization

It addresses strategies for minimizing film waste and optimizing costs throughout the silage production process. It provides practical tips for achieving optimal film coverage while minimizing overlaps and gaps. The chapter also highlights the importance of training and educating personnel involved in film application to reduce human errors and improve efficiency. Additionally, it explores cost-saving measures such as bulk film purchasing, inventory management, and strategic timing of film orders to take advantage of price fluctuations.

9.4 Automation and Technological Innovations

This section explores the role of automation and technological innovations in enhancing operational efficiency. It discusses advancements such as automated wrapping systems, computerized controls, and remote monitoring capabilities. The chapter highlights the benefits of these technologies in terms of time savings, labor optimization, and improved process control. Readers will gain insights into the potential of automation and technological innovations to streamline silage production and storage operations.

9.5 Best Practices for Silage Storage and Handling

This chapter concludes with a focus on best practices for silage storage and handling that significantly contribute to operational efficiency. It discusses proper stacking, space utilization, and ventilation techniques to ensure optimal airflow and minimize spoilage. The chapter also highlights the importance of regular monitoring, sampling, and feedout practices to maintain silage quality throughout the feeding period. Readers will learn actionable insights into the key considerations and practical tips that ensure efficient silage storage and handling, thereby optimizing overall farm operations.

By addressing the critical aspect of operational efficiency, Chapter 9 provides valuable guidance for dairy business owners and livestock producers. The chapter emphasizes the importance of selecting the right silage film, implementing efficient film application techniques, minimizing waste, and leveraging automation and technological innovations. Implementing these strategies enhances overall operational efficiency, reduces costs, and optimizes silage production processes.

○   ○   ○   ○

CHAPTER 10

The Essential Role of Silage Repair Tape

Silage preservation is a delicate process, and maintaining the integrity of your silage cover is essential to ensuring high-quality, nutrient-rich feed for your livestock. A crucial but often overlooked tool in this process is silage repair tape. This specialized adhesive tape plays a vital role in sealing leaks, tears, and other damages that could compromise the silage pile or bunker.

10.1 What is Silage Repair Tape?

Silage repair tape is a heavy-duty, weather-resistant adhesive material designed to quickly and effectively seal holes, punctures, and rips in silage covers. The tape is typically made from a combination of strong polyethylene or PVC materials with a highly adhesive backing, allowing it to bond securely to both the silage film and the silage pile itself, .

10.2 Why is Silage Repair Tape Important?

10.2.1 Preventing Air and Water Exposure:

Any gap or hole in your silage cover can introduce air and water, which drastically reduce the quality of the silage. The introduction of oxygen leads to unwanted aerobic fermentation, causing spoilage and loss of nutrients. Silage repair tape helps seal these gaps to maintain an airtight environment and preserve the silage's nutritional value.

10.2.2 Saving Time and Money:

Rather than replacing entire sections of damaged silage film or cover, you can use silage repair tape to quickly address issues and continue your operation without delays. This cost-effective solution can save both time and money in the long run, ensuring the silage is properly preserved without the need for costly, time-consuming repairs.

10.2.3 Durability and Weather Resistance:

Silage repair tape is specifically designed to withstand harsh weather conditions, including exposure to UV rays, rain, and fluctuating temperatures. This ensures the repairs stay intact, and your silage remains properly preserved even under adverse weather conditions, reducing the risk of spoilage.

10.2.4 Easy Application:

The beauty of silage repair tape lies in its simplicity. It's easy to apply and doesn't require specialized training. You can quickly patch up damaged areas of the silage cover with minimal effort, restoring its integrity and ensuring continued preservation.

10.3 How to Use Silage Repair Tape

10.3.1 Identify the Damage:

First, inspect your silage cover for any tears, punctures, or damage. This can be done manually or by using a visual inspection tool, such as a drone for larger silage piles.

10.3.2 Clean the Area:

Make sure the area around the tear or puncture is clean and dry. Dirt, moisture, or debris can prevent the tape from adhering properly, so it's essential to prepare the surface for a strong bond.

10.3.3 Apply the Tape:

Cut the required length of silage repair tape and apply it directly over the damaged area. Press down firmly to ensure a secure seal. Be sure to cover the entire tear, and slightly overlap the edges to create a robust, airtight seal.

10.3.4 Check the Seal:

After applying the tape, check to ensure the repair is holding firmly. It's a good practice to recheck the seal after a few hours and during periodic maintenance to make sure the tape remains intact.

10.4 Types of Silage Repair Tape

There are various types of silage repair tapes available in the market, each suited for different needs. Common types include:

➢ **Standard Repair Tape:** Ideal for small holes and rips in silage covers.

➢ **Heavy-Duty Repair Tape:** Designed for larger, more significant damage that requires extra reinforcement and durability.

➢ **UV-Resistant Tape:** Best for areas exposed to high amounts of sunlight, as it won't degrade or lose adhesion over time.

➢ **Reflective Repair Tape:** For higher visibility in low-light conditions, helping workers spot damage more easily.

Common Applications for Silage Repair Tape

➢ **Cover Repairs:** Whether you're dealing with a tear in your plastic wrap or a puncture in your silage bag, silage repair tape is the go-to solution for effective repairs.

➢ **Sealing Small Holes in Bunkers:** Even minor gaps in bunker silos can lead to significant spoilage, making repair tape essential for maintaining silage quality.

➢ **Emergency Repairs:** In case of unexpected damage, silage repair tape offers a quick fix, enabling you to preserve the silage without waiting for professional help.

○   ○   ○   ○

CHAPTER 11

Success Stories:
Case Studies in Silage Film Application

This chapter explores a series of real-life case studies that illustrate the challenges faced by dairy farmers and livestock producers when using silage film and how these challenges were overcome. Each case study focuses on a specific problem and highlights the solutions implemented using silage film. The chapter features characters who represent actual customers and their experiences. By examining these success stories, readers will gain insights into the practical applications of silage film and its profound impact on addressing common issues faced in the industry. The chapter is divided into the following sections:

11.1 Case Study 1: Maximizing Forage Preservation for Mr. Singh's Dairy Farm

Character: Mr. Singh - Dairy Farmer

Problem: Mr. Singh was facing difficulties in achieving optimal forage preservation due to exposure to air and spoilage. This resulted in reduced nutrient content and overall feed quality.

Solution: Through the implementation of a specific type of high-quality silage film, combined with proper wrapping techniques, Mr. Singh was able to maximize forage preservation. The film's superior barrier properties created an airtight environment, significantly reducing spoilage and nutrient losses.

Outcome: By using the recommended silage film, Mr. Singh observed improved forage quality, increased feed efficiency, and enhanced animal performance. The higher nutritional content of the preserved forage resulted in healthier cows and improved farm profitability.

11.2 Case Study 2: Ensuring Feed Availability During Seasonal Variation for Mrs. Patel's Livestock Farm

Character: Mrs. Patel - Livestock Producer

Problem: Mrs. Patel faced challenges in maintaining a consistent feed supply during periods of seasonal variation in forage production. This led to potential shortages and compromised animal nutrition.

Solution: By employing strategic silage film usage and proper storage techniques, Mrs. Patel was able to preserve surplus forage for future use. The high-quality silage film effectively sealed the silage, protecting it from external elements and ensuring its availability during lean seasons.

Outcome: Mrs. Patel achieved a reliable and continuous feed supply throughout the year, mitigating the impact of seasonal variations. This resulted in improved animal health, steady milk production, and enhanced profitability for her livestock farm.

11.3 Case Study 3: Minimizing Nutrient Losses and Improving Animal Health for Mr. Khan's Cattle Ranch

Character: Mr. Khan - Cattle Ranch Owner

Problem: Mr. Khan encountered excessive nutrient losses in his silage due to inadequate preservation methods, leading to compromised animal health and reduced productivity.

Solution: By adopting a comprehensive silage management plan that included the use of high-performance silage film, Mr. Khan successfully minimized nutrient losses. The film's exceptional oxygen barrier properties and UV resistance protected the forage, preserving its nutrient content and overall quality.

Outcome: Mr. Khan witnessed significant improvements in animal health, including reduced instances of digestive issues and enhanced feed conversion. The high-quality silage resulted in increased milk production, healthier cattle, and improved profitability for his cattle ranch.

Each case study within ;this chapter highlights a specific problem faced by the customer and demonstrates how the implementation of proper silage film solutions effectively addressed those challenges. By showcasing these success stories, readers gain practical, real-world insights into the benefits of silage film for maximizing forage preservation, ensuring feed availability, minimizing nutrient losses, and improving overall animal health.

$$\circ \quad \circ \quad \circ \quad \circ$$

Conclusion

As we reach the end of **"SILAGE MASTERY: REDUCE WASTE, MAXIMISE MILK PRODUCTION, AND BOOST DAIRY EFFICIENCY,"** I want to express my sincere gratitude for joining me on this journey of exploring the profound impact of silage film on the dairy industry. Throughout this book, we have delved into the intricacies of silage preservation, the importance of high-quality film, and the strategies for achieving optimal results in dairy operations.

It is evident that silage film plays a crucial role in ensuring the preservation and nutritional value of silage, which directly translates into higher milk production and increased profitability for dairy farmers. By employing advanced film techniques and incorporating industry best practices, farmers can harness the power of silage film to unlock the full potential of their dairy businesses.

We have covered a wide range of topics from the different types of silage film and manufacturing processes to the critical considerations for selecting the right film for specific farm needs. Additionally, we have examined the science behind UV stabilization, additives, and the innovative technology of printed silage film, which opens up new avenues for branding and marketing within the industry.

Throughout this book, we have also delved into real-life case studies that illustrate the challenges faced by dairy farmers and how they successfully overcome them using proper silage film techniques. These stories serve as inspiring examples of how strategic implementation and attention to detail can lead to remarkable results.

It is my sincere hope that the knowledge, insights, and practical guidance shared in this book have equipped you with the tools necessary to optimize your dairy productivity, enhance animal health, and ultimately, elevate the success of your dairy business. By leveraging the power of silage film and embracing innovation, you can position yourself at the forefront of the industry and achieve sustainable growth.

I would like to express my deepest appreciation to all the individuals who have contributed to the creation of this book, from the dairy farmers and industry professionals who generously shared their experiences to the experts and researchers who have dedicated their lives to advancing the field of silage preservation. Your collective efforts have made this book possible, and I am truly humbled by the opportunity to share your knowledge with others.

I encourage you to continue exploring and embracing the latest advancements in silage film technology. Stay updated on cutting-edge research and industry trends. The journey towards optimizing dairy productivity is an ongoing one, and by staying informed and adaptable, you can continue to drive progress and achieve greater success in your dairy operations.

Once again, I extend my heartfelt gratitude to you, the readers, for your interest, dedication, and passion for the dairy industry.

It is my sincerest wish that "Silage Solutions: Optimising Dairy Productivity with Advanced Film Techniques" serves as a valuable resource and guide on your path to unlocking the full potential of your dairy business.

Wishing you continued success, prosperity, and growth in all your endeavors.

○   ○   ○   ○

Take the Leap!

Loved reading Silage Mastery?

Take your learning further....

Are you dealing with following challenges?

➢ Addressing issues with silage film breaking down due to UV light?

➢ Overcoming credit challenges and exploring alternate solutions?

➢ Managing pricing concerns, especially during peak seasons?

Don't Worry, We have the perfect solutions here...

We invite you to book a personalized consultation with our expert

Who has 35+ years of experience and serving...

720+ Companies | 52 bl. meter film | 8+ Countries

To schedule your one-to-one session, simply scan this QR Code is

Don't miss this opportunity to take
your business to next level!